MY TESTIMONY

FROM DEATH DOOR TO LIFE

Evangelist Beverly A Swinson

authorHOUSE®

AuthorHouse™
1663 Liberty Drive
Bloomington, IN 47403
www.authorhouse.com
Phone: 1-800-839-8640

First published by AuthorHouse 1/31/2011

ISBN: 978-1-4567-2401-6 (e)
ISBN: 978-1-4567-2402-3 (sc)

Library of Congress Control Number: 2011900062

Printed in the United States of America

ABOUT THE AUTHOR
BEVERLY ANN SWINSON

Beverly started in church at the early age of nine with her three cousins under the direction of their grandmother the late Rev Essie Williams. Beverly and her mother along with her grandmother joined New Hope Free Will Baptist Church in Washington DC. In the early 70's Beverly attended Woodson Jr. High School. Beverly transferred from Woodson Jr. High School to Hines Jr. High School this was where she spent her last two years studying music and secretarial skills before moving on to high school. While attending Hines Jr. High she joined the Hines Jazz Band where she performed around the Washington DC Metropolitan area and in school along with her school band mates. Beverly participated in the Washington DC talent search at the Boys and Girls Club at the encouragement of her band teacher. Beverly performed in the talent search and from that show she was asked to audition with Orpheus Band and Show. Beverly stayed with Orpheus for three years while attending high school from 1978 thru 1980 the band performed various parks in the Washington DC area during the summer months along with other bands that are well known to this day. After the bands broke up due to Band members going off to College Beverly joined the military in 1980 she served until 1986 then she rejoined the military in 2000 where she deployed to Fort Dix Army training base during the start of the Iraqi war in 2003 she song with the Fort Dix Chapel choir while station there I am now an Evangelist in my church.

INTRODUCTION

THE LORD HAS INSPIRED ME TO WRITE MY LIFE TESTIMONY, THIS IS NOT A STORY, IT'S A TESTIMONY HOW GOD HAS SEEN ME THROUGH THE TRIALS OF LIFE, I AM STILL HERE TO TESTIFY OF THE GOODNESS OF JESUS CHRIST, WHO IS THE HEAD OF MY LIFE, THE LOVER OF MY SOUL, AND THE PROVIDER THAT NO MAN CAN TOUCH. HE ALLOWED ME TO SAY (GOD CAN DO IT) I AM WRITING ON THE INSPIRATION OF GOD'S ANOINTING POWER ONLY BECAUSE I CAN NOT DO ANYTHING ON MY OWN. I DO NOT KNOW THE REASON FOR THE BIRTHING OF THIS BOOK, ONLY GOD HAS THAT ANSWER; I 'M JUST AN INSTRUMENT WHICH HE CAN WORK THROUGH. GOD SAW IT WAS GOOD FOR ME TO LIVE, HE HAS DEPOSITED ANOINTING ON MY LIFE TO

GO AND SHARE HIS GOOD NEWS OF JESUS CHRIST TO TELL THAT HE LIVES AND HE IS STILL WORKING MIRACLES TO DAY. I PRAY THAT THIS BOOK WILL TOUCH SOMEONE'S LIFE THAT IT WILL BRING THE FRUITS OF SALVATION, A HEALING OF DELIVERANCE, AND A HEALING OF HOPE. GODS HOLY ANOINTING IS AN IMPACT ON OUR LIVIES IT SENDS US INTO A METAMORPHOSIS STAGE. WHAT I MEAN, IT'S A CONSTANT CHANGE. BEFORE THE CHANGE CAN TAKE PLACE, THERE IS A TIME WHEN IT FEELS LIKE EVERYTHING STOPS. NOTHING IS HAPPENING, JOB LOST, CHRISTIAN FRIENDS DON'T COME AROUND, EVEN FAMILY STAYS AWAY, BE NOT IN DISPARE GOD IS WORKING EVERYTHING OUT ON OUR BEHALF AND GOD IS IN CONTROL A BIRTHING IS TAKING PLACE, OR A CONCEPTION IS GOING ON. LIKE CHILD BIRTH IT'S PAINFUL, GOD HAD ESTABLISHED IT FROM THE FOUNDATION OF THE WORLD.

HOLD ON, IT IS COMING FORTH, BOOK, PROPHECY MINISTRY, SONG, OR etc.......... SALVATION, DELIVERANE, HEALING IT WILL SOON MAKE ITS WAY THROUGH THE SPIRITUAL BIRTH CANAL.

DEDICATION

I WANT TO DEDICATE THIS BOOK FIRST TO ALMIGHTY GOD, HIS SON JESUS CHRIST, AND THE HOLY SPIRIT WHO HAS INSPIRED ME TO WRITE THIS BOOK.

TO MY MOTHER WHOM I LOVE AND APPRECIATE MRS, BEATRICE WILLIAMS DARDEN WHO CARRIED ME AND ALLOWED ME TO BE HERE WITH THE HELP OF GOD. TO MY GRANDMOTHER THE LATE REV. ESSIE UDELL WILLIAMS, MAY GOD REST HER SANCTIFIED SOUL, WHO GAVE ME THE LESSONS OF THIS SPIRITUAL LIVING, WHO ANOINTED MY HEAD AND READ THE WORD OF GOD TO ME WHILE I STAY WITH HER. TO MY AUNTS AND UNCLES AND COUSINS WHO LABOR IN THE WORD OF GOD TO MY COUSIN REV. LEROY WILLIAMS WHO I GREW UP WITH; HIS SINGING INSPIRED ME SO MUCH. TO MY

SISTERS WHOM GOD GAVE TO ME, I WAS AN ONLY CHILD FOR TWELVE YEARS. TO MY BEAUTI FUL CHILDREN **I LOVE YOU BOTH VERY MUCH, MOMMY.** TO MRS. GWENDOLIN FRANCES WHO GOD PUT IN MY PATH TO WITNESS TO, SHE HAS BEEN A STRONG FRIEND IN MY LIFE AND HER HUSBAND HEROLD THANKS, FOR BEING MY GOD GIVEN FRIENDS **LOVE BEV.** APPRECIATION GOES OUT TO THE LORD HOUSE OF GLORY , CHAPLAIN AND OVERSEER RONALD MACK AND HIS FIRST LADY AND WIFE TONI MACK WHO ENCOURAGED ME TO SEEK GOD FOR THE WEALTH THAT IS STORED UP INSIDE OF ME, CHAPLAIN SAY'S **"IT'S IN SIDE OF YOU LET IT OUT GO ON LET IT OUT." LOL!** THANK YOU.

TO THE PASTOR OF TRIBE OF JUDAH, WHO HEARD THE VOICE OF GOD AND OBEYED HIM WHERE I WAS FIRST ORDAINED AS AN EVANGELIST, THANK YOU FOR HEARING GOD. TO ALL OF THE PASTORS WHO BROUGHT FORTH THE WORD OF GOD THAT HELPED SHAPE ME INTO THE MINISTER THAT GOD CALLED ME TO BE. THE BISHOP OF BIBLEWAY CHURCH IN GOD IN CHRIST

IN CINCINNATI OHIO, TO THE LATE BISHOP AND HIS FIRST LADY THE APOSTLE OF JERICHO CITY OF PRAISE WORSHIP CENTER, MAY THE LORD CONTINUALLY USE YOU FOR HIS GLORY. THANK YOU ALL! GOD HAS ALLOWED YOU TO BE THE INSTRUMENT TO SHAPE MY LIFE.

CHAPTER ONE

From Death Door To Life

First to the only wise and living God who is the head of my life and the keeper of my soul

Hello, allow me to introduce myself my name is Beverly Ann Swinson, I was born in Goldsboro North Carolina, on Septemember 20, 1962 to the late Eddy Lee Worrall's, and Beatrice Williams at that time, since then mother has remarried and now her last name is Darden. I was delivered in a house on Popular Street, by a midwife. My mother was a young woman and was not able to afford hospital treatment; my mother married my father she had many trials to endure during their marriage. Mother had to put up with his drinking as well his sleeping around with other women. With these actions her life with him was hard. My father's responsibility for his family was not his main focus. Mother had to work hard on her own to make ends meet at times there wasn't enough in the house for us to eat, so I didn't get fed properly she had to borrow food from others so I could eat, sometimes mother didn't eat herself so I could. The house we lived in didn't have much heat at times, mother kept on traveling to do what she knew how to do, these living conditions caused me to become sick with pneumonia, mother thought it was just a cold and she treated it as such. My condition worsened as days and nights went on, I wasn't able to breathe properly mother and another family member rush me to the doctor where I was seen and examined and the doctor discovered I had pneumonia. The pneumonia had sat in both of my lungs that caused my immune system to become weak. The doctor put me in the hospital he told mother that he didn't believed I was going to make it through, they put me in what look like a bubble bed, a bed that was covered with plastic "say's my mother." The doctor did all they knew how at this point.

I was only nine month's old suffering with double pneumonia in both lugs. **(But God!)** It was going to take a miracle if I was going to live. In the 60's there wasn't good technology like today's technology. I could have died as time went on God seen it was good to keep me here. (Hallelujah!) God gave me to a family that knew him and knew how to pray God even knew this was going to happen. My grandmother was a preacher; her father was a traveling Evangelist God rests their souls. The anointing of God was already on my life quiet as it was kept. God can take life away or he can let it remain. I give God praise for my life without him I'm nothing, in him I live, and in him I have my being. I made it through that storm at the beginning of my life and there were many more to come not knowing this as a baby girl. **Scripture References Genesis 2:7 and the Lord God formed man of the dust of the ground and breathe into his nostrils the breath of life and man became a living soul.**

HABIT NOT TAKEN

There was a another time in my life God has kept me this one was when my father used to take me with him to his aunt's house, this lady use to sell liquor made from corn husk, they call it corn liquor the guys including my father use to go there after work to wind down before going home, and the weekends hang out. My mother told me "my father use to come and get me and take me with him to his aunt's house and sat me on his knee while he was drinking, and he would order me a glass of beer". Estimating my age between 2 to 4years old. My father enjoyment in life was drinking unfortunately in time it took over his life; he had connection, his mother's sister, he could walk right out of his front door right into his aunt's back door that's how close his liquor store was.

Daddy would pick me up from my mother's house to spend time with me (some time right!). "One day my mother saw daddy and I walking up the road he had snuck me out of the house while she was at work this day we both where stumbling trying to walk, daddy would take two steps back and one step up, and I was falling down and getting back up again trying to walk." **LOL!** This made mother angry with him, mother grabbed me and took me home and allowed me to sleep. The outcome of this mother knew in her heart that if she didn't stop him while I was young I would have taken on this habit of his. **But God!** She stopped him from coming over to get me to take me anywhere, she would leave me with another of her family members that he didn't know of so these activities finally stopped. My little system did not crave any of that taste, right now to this day I cannot stand the taste of beer. **Look how God works!**

As I sit here in my apartment quietly seeking God for something in my life it comes to this Book. Remember **HOLD ON DELIVERANC IS NEAR TO YOU! Scripture Reference: Psalm 121:5 The Lord is thy keeper: the Lord is thy shade upon thy right hand.**

ELECTROCUTION STYLE

As I grew my mother left my biological father and North Carolina she settled here in Washington DC on Small Street just off of Pennsylvania Avenue known today as Capitol Hill.

Mother took a job cleaning house it was not much but it was enough to help purchase food and keep the heat on, she rented a small apartment room upstairs in an apartment house where a friend that new my mother lived.

The upstairs had a living room, kitchen, bathroom, and a bed room, small but nice I was six years old. I had a little toy TV that was called **SHOW- N- TELL TELEVISION** this toy played records and it even had a place on it to put in slides to show different pictures while listening to the record. Well one night while my mother and her gentleman friend was in the living room I was to stay in our room where my mother and I shared space. I remember playing with my TV toy and as I was playing with it I went to unplug the thing, I could not get it loose it was plug in to a drop cord socket instead of waiting for my mother to do it for me I put the drop cord in my mouth, and bit down on it (Whoooo!) I got electrocuted, seeing stars, lights of color, and my hair even stood up on top of my head (Good God O' Mighty LOL!)

God is good, I was screaming and crying my mother and her gentleman friend ran in the room to see what had happen. It was not life threatening, nor was it to the point I needed medical treatment, but it just shook me up there was not enough volts to cause that much damage thank God, mother attended to my wound, then she says to me I'm not going to spank you for this because this has given you what you need already. Again I give this scripture reference. **Psalm121:5 The Lord is thy keeper: the Lord is thy shade upon thy right hand.** Like unto this accident we sometimes go on our own Accord and do things not pleasing unto God, trying to do things in our own way so the electrocution of life electrocutes us, some time it does lead to death, but with God's grace and mercy it does not. Some electricity carries from 90% to a 1000% or higher volts depending on how much current it is holding. I believe God said before he place me in my mother's womb let me give this girl some resistance of life, he already knew I was going to get into things that would cause me pain. God keeps death back from us so we can strive to get it right. Sometime's God does not punish us because of that very thing we get ourselves into will give us the shock of our lives, God loves us so he just mends our wounds when we are hurting, even when we are wrong, like mother mending my wound knew that I was wrong. Some may say the enemy had me to do that, it may be so but I believe it was an act of disobedience not waiting for my mother to help me. It was just a bad choice on my part we do make bad choices in life that can electrocute you and cause a wound that need s to be mended but God is the only one who can mend those kind of wounds. Through this experience God saw that it was good to keep me here still **(HALLELUJAH!) I SAY STOP! DON'T DO IT! TELL GOD ABOUT IT FRIST!**

RUNNING INTO A WALL

At the age of nine, half of the Williams family had settled here in Washington DC and the New Jersey area to live. My grandparents, my aunts, uncles and their children. As I remember my grandparents stayed on G Street NE right off of H Street they live in an apartment house on the top floor just like my mother but on the other side of Pennsylvania Ave. Back in the day the landlord lived on the top floor of the house they owned a two level house. They made their home into two parts, separating the top floor from the bottom. They rented out the top space as an apartment. The person owning the home always lived on the bottom floor, they were my grandparent's landlords. My grandparent's live three doors down from my aunt's husband's cousin's house she and her husband, lived in an actual apartment building that was stationed in the middle of G Street this apartment building was built next to a cement wall that divided the apartment house from this actual apartment. As I can recall in this moment of my quite time, my aunt and her husband who is from New Jersey and their children were visiting with us, at my aunt's who had taken care of my ear. Her husband cousin's house, which lived next door to my grandparents on the other side of that cement wall at her apartment. My Aunt had five children two of them were boys they loved basketball. They hoped to be pro ball players one day. Well they are now preachers just like their dad as of this day. That day when they were visiting the boys were outside playing catch and I wanted to play too. They let me play the game one would throw the ball and the other one had to catch the ball, guess who had to catch the ball, **(me)** of course, I stood in front of this cement wall because there was not enough ground space where the building stood, so we played there on the front as I reach out to catch the ball that was being thrown to me, the ball was landing down by the wall over my head, the sun glared my vision and I wasn't able to see where the ball was going. I turned and was met with this cement wall hitting it with my forehead, it tore a hole in the middle of my forehead, and blood started to run down my face covering my eyes, it knocked me down, but it didn't knock me out. The boys picked me up and carried me into the apartment where all the adults were. My mother said, Lord what has this girl gotten into now. The boys told her what had happen she replied to me girl you know better than playing with these boys you know they are too rough for you. Again mother attended to my wound and patched me up thank God the wound was not deep enough that I needed stitches. It healed over time, for a long time I carried a small scare in the middle of my forehead as I have gotten older the scar just got smaller. My friends just think if God's grace had not been there it would have been worse than it was. Again, **BUT GOD!** In our lives we are going to be with someone or around people that will set you up to run into a cement wall that will tear a hole in your forehead of life, as you are standing wounded with a hole in your head remember God's love, and grace is sufficient for thee. God will patch you up, and in time it will heal. **HOLD ON YOUR ARE BEING KNOCKED DOWN, BUT YOU ARE NOT KNOCKED OUT. II Corinthians 12:9 and he said unto me, my grace is sufficient for thee: for my strength is made perfect in weakness. Most gladly therefore will I rather glory in my infirmities, that the power of Christ may rest upon me. Psalm 121:5 The Lord is thy keeper: the Lord is thy shade upon thy right hand.**

PAIN IN MY EAR

In this year not only did I have a head blow knock down event, I was not hearing so clearly because there was a pain in my ear. I had another body drama, I was babysitting my younger cousins who were 4 1/2 and 5 years old my aunt's daughters, she worked as an X-ray Tech at Howard University hospital, she worked the night shift. She asks my mother could I sit with the girls because my cousin that is mush older had gone out on a date. Well this is not so much life threatening, but it did cause much pain in my ear. My ears are the only thing that I have to hear with, my cousins and I were bedding down for the night my aunt their mother had not left for work. Back in the day siblings of the same sex had to share bed space at times depending on how large the living quarters were or how many beds there were. The girls and I had our own beds we just love to share space in their mother's bed while she was out. Ok moving on, as we were in bed looking at television as we use to say TV, I was going to clean my ear with a Q'tip I left the Q'tip in my left ear and laid down on the opposite side pulling the sheet over top of the Q'tip, it jugged down in my ear I quickly pulled it out of my ear and blood just started to flow down my neck. The girls were screaming from seeing the blood, and I was crying from the pain in my ear. My aunt had not left for work yet, she rushed in the room to see what had happen, trying to stop the bleeding she push cotton balls in my ear and she rushed me to the hospital, then she called my mother. Again mama said "girl you are going to kill yourself if you don't stop. Between playing with those boys what am I going to do with you?" One minute please I have to sit back and laugh at myself **(LOL!)** God has been good to me! Even though this episode was not life threatening it caused a heap of pain in my ear for at least a month, as it healed it seemed like the pain got worse eventually it did heal. **Matthew 13: 16 but bless are your eyes for they see: and your ears, for they hear.** I say we must watch what we allow to enter into our ears for they are the instrument of hearing others gross conversation, talking about others negatively and loud up notches noise that has no meaning loud music, this kind of thing can cause pain in your spiritual ear just imaged that someone was cursing you out and that sound got stuck in your ear I believe it would be painful to keep hearing that loud gross conversation over and over again. This can cause pain to your physical ear as well as your spiritual ear.

STAY IN A QUIET ATMOSPHERE TO HEAR ONLY GOD

CHAPTER TWO

Some Thing Taken From Me

Growing up is sometimes painful and not good. As I reached puberty growing into a young lady between ten or eleven years old I was surrounded by another set of family members. My mother's brother children. At times I was left with my cousins, while mother and my Uncle and his wife would go out on the town. He was my mother's as she would say "my favorite brother." I was left with my cousins the middle girl even though she was older than me she still loved to play with her dolls, as we did often on many occasion. One day or evening there was a change in the atmosphere; she was called out of the house by one of her friends that lived two doors down. During her absence the younger brother came in the room and said to me with an anxious voice he had something to show me so I must come with him. We started down the stairs toward the basement of their house he was a little bit ahead of me and as I reach the bottom of the stairs he was standing in front of an opening that was draped with curtains so it would look like a room. He said come here, it is right over here.

As I approached the entrance way he ran pass me and just after that so quickly his older brother grabbed me and pushed me down on this mattress that was in the place behind this curtain. Here is where my virginity was taken away from me, it hurt me so it felt like my soul was been taking away from me. **(Rape some will call it, incest others will say)** but God calls it sin that stink up into his nostril. **(Oh God Who!)** Excuse me please while I breathe! This cut me to my soul as time went on he was telling me if I told anybody he would say that I was messing with him and they would believe him first before they would believe me.

At any given time when he would catch me by myself or sometime he would go pick his girl friend up from work and ask if I could ride with him, he would stop off in the cemetery and would proceed raping me again there in the car. At this time something came over me, I was tired of him plunging me I started to fight back to make him stop.

He eventually did stop I couldn't find it in myself to tell anyone not even my mother because he was the child of her favorite brother so this has stayed with me half of my teen and adult life. **(BUT GOD!)** I want to stop here for a moment to share some scriptures; I give this no place in my life.

Proverbs 28:10 Whoso causes the righteous to go astray in an evil way, he shall fall himself into his own pit: but the upright shall have good things in possession. Proverbs 28:17 A man that doeth violence to the blood of any person shall flee to the pit: let no man stay him. As I continue to grow into womanhood I continued to cover this mess up for years. It began to feel like it was not there anymore; I covered it up with a boy friend that I met while in North Carolina for a summer vacation from school.

I got caught by staying out too late with him at the school ground , and his house, yes we had sex that was my plan he fell right into the plan him not knowing what was on my mind. Getting caught was not in the plan but we did. When it was over my mother was furious with me she was to come down and pick me up before the summer was over. This was suppose to have cut my summer vacation short, instead she had my step father's brother in law take me from my aunt's house and keep me with him at his house. He had two girl of his own my

15

cousins on my step father's side. He was a big tall man he was strict on his girls they could not go hardly anywhere unless he took them. So I was with them until my mother came for me as she did. At this time I was between twelve or thirteen. By the time my mother came to get me her anger had lessened, she was concern about me being with child at a young age. I'm going to cut this short, she took me to the Doctor and I was given birth control pills, to save me from my own ungodly mistake. Really where was my action stemming from I found myself going from one relationship to another wanting someone, every boy and man to except me but all I was getting in return was just the sex act no real exceptions I was lying to myself feeling rejected after a relationship had broken up and the pain just came back again I remember saying to myself once I'm cursed because my relationships were not lasting to where I felt I should had been excepted **(BUT GOD!)**. I was obedient to my mother by taken those pills every day. Hey this is a lot to take in from one person I know, I can take it deeper but God only wants me to inspirer and to encourage somebody with this testimony so I am going to stop for now ok. Just take a moment to think about someone who had taken away something so precious from you it just tore a hole in your soul, it could be anything or anyone and it just feels like it touches your soul.

There are people that are assigned to your life to do

just that, it can hurt you so that you take another road that will change the course of your life, until the Master touches you with his loving power. This happened to me but the change came at a later date in my life read on you will see the change. I want to encourage you with this the Book of Job Chapter two God gave Satan just enough power to strict Job to prove that Job had it in him to survive the deepest of the deepest tragedy that any man can bare. Job had the strength to wait on God for a change in his sedation. God is in control of everything he only allows things to happen for his Glory only.

TO GOD BE ALL THE GLORY! Psalm 46:1 God is our refuge and strength, a very present help trouble. I say God is near right now no matter what the test, be bold, be strong for the Lord thy God is with thee

CHAPTER THREE

Push A Side, Had To Fight, Not For Gotten

During my junior high school years my mother got remarried to a man who I now call my father my biological father still lived in North Carolina his drinking had taken over his life, and mother did not want me to have no part of him. So my mother's new husband put his name on my birth certificate he gave me his last name, mother said it was easy to do because my biological father never put his name on my birth certificate. Now he is the man I call father. Junior high school was hard for me because I had a learning disorder, for real I just could not read this caused me to be push aside by my teachers because they didn't want to help or they did not have the time. I remember back in the 3rd grade, I heard the teacher telling my mother that I had learning problems, I was too slow and she didn't have the time to teach me what I didn't know. She had to help those children that already knew how to read and do math. Mother took me out of that school, for the summer I was place in another school in the next school year mother purchased the world book encyclopedia that came with learning tools that could help me to spell, read, and do math. My mother had me at the kitchen table every chance she could, with the learning tools that she had purchased, so I could at least come up to a learning speed that would place me with the other children. So the teacher would at least put me with the others that were a bit faster than me. I wasn't the only child in school that had this problem the teacher would put us in groups, the faster learning children she taught, and our group was left alone to play until she came to a part that she knew we knew how to do.

Getting back to junior high school this brings me to tell about when I was attending Woodson Junior High School, this was the roughest year that I had ever had since elementary school. My peers were fighting me; teacher didn't have the time to teach me because I didn't get the hang of the reading portion down. Again I was pushed aside, the teacher felt like at this point I should have known how to read and do math, well because of the past the teacher just passed me along to get rid of me. In junior high school they gave me something else to do when it came to a part of the lesson that I could not do or keep up. On the other hand the girls in school didn't care for me because I didn't hang out with the drinking or smoking group, this was a problem. The girls would pick fights with me, one day this girl and I fought from the cafeteria. One time mother had to pick me up from school because the girls were going to jump me. Mother is the fighter I didn't like to fight but did only if I was provoked. While we were riding home from school she rode pass the girls that wanted to jump me. Mother drove the car right in front of them and she got out of the car and approached them, saying you are not going to jump her. If you still just want to fight her they were only going to do it one by one. She was going to make me fight them. Mother was bad and didn't take any stuff off any body, as small as she was. It's just like God He comes to our defense when Satan and his imps are trying to overpower us. God sends out his fighting war angels to help us in times of trouble, God say if there is to be a fight my children fight only with my word and the Armor. Put on the whole armor of God that we may be able to stand against the wiles of the devil. **II Corinthians 6:7 by the word of truth, by the power of God, by the amour of righteousness on the right hand and on the left. I Timothy 6: 12 Fight the good fight** of faith , lay hold on eternal life, whereunto thou art also called, and hast professed a good profession before many witnesses.

II Timothy 4:7 I have fought a good fight, I have finished my course, I have kept the faith. Ephesians 6:11-18 Put on the whole armour of God that ye may be able to stand against the wiles of the devil. For we wrestle not against flesh and blood, but against powers, against the rulers of the darkness of this world, against spiritual wickedness in high places. Wherefore take unto you the whole armor of God that ye may be able to with stand in the evil day, and having done all, to stand. Stand therefore, having your loins girt abut with truth and having on the breastplate of righteousness. And your feet shod with the preparation of the gospel of peace. Above all, taking the shield of faith, wherewith ye shall be able to quench all the fiery darts of the wicked. And take the helmet of salvation and the sword of the spirit, which is the word of God: Praying always with all prayer and supplication in the spirit and watching thereunto with all perseverance and supplication for all saints; God has a plan there was a special person that God place in my path while I was attending this school Woodson. This person was low key, laid back, not seen much, but every once and a while he would come to each class to talk with the teachers. I remember my math teacher had a conference with my mother, her name was

Miss Watson very nice lady, she introduce my mother to this laid back, not seen much man, he had a meeting with my mother, he told her he was a special Ed teacher, and he specializes in teaching children how to read and do math. **(GOD HAS A PLAN!)** My teacher put my name on the list for his class for two hours during the regular class time, to work with me on my reading. But he could not do anything unless he got permission from my mother so, mother agreed he prepared papers for my mother to sign. I started going to his class for two hours during school time. When I came to his class it was a room that use to be use by the school janitor, where they used to store cleaning items, this room was turned in to a small reading area, there were two desk in this room, his disk and the student desk, papers and books were everywhere. This man thought me how to read and do math I could keep up in class. Now I am able to write this book with God's inspiring power. He is still doing his thing; he is a counsel in youth juvenile system. **(I THANK GOD FOR HIM)** We met up three years ago and I just could not thank him enough. He said to me, Beverly he even remembered my name you already knew how to read, but you didn't believe you could. I just help you to know that you could, **(WOW!)** that was a powerful statement I stood there and started to shed some tears, he just wipe my eyes and said it's ok, so how are you. I started sharing some brief up dates with him and the good things in my life. He started to shed some tears too, It's so good to know I was still alive to see him again, because some of the others I went to school with are deceased . Mother took me out of Woodson Junior High School because it was getting too rough she was tired of me fighting. We moved to the northeast side of Washington DC, in the area we use to live, when we first came to Washington DC this side of town is now know n as, Capitol Hill. I graduated from Hine Junior High School and went on to Chamberlain High School where I graduated in the year 1981. **Ephesians 6:12 for we wrestle not against flesh and blood, but principality against powers, against the rulers of the darkness of this world, against spiritual wickedness in high place.**

CHAPTER FOUR

The Fire And The Gun

The fire started by the door. As a young woman growing into adulthood, I remember dating and partying just having a good time as I thought at this time of my life. One time I was dating this older man and like my biological father he turned to liquor for his pleasure along with sex, we had been out at a club, we were having a good time and my boy friend became tore down, (meaning) drunk. He became so drunk that I had to drive him home, somehow I managed to get him into his apartment, and I didn't go home that night I stayed with him. I was getting him settled in for the night I managed to get him into bed, helping him out of his clothing, making things comfortable for us. He had one room efficiency; it was only a one room apartment with only one way out. The windows had bars on them because he lived on the ground floor so the bars were protection from break-ins. After we had settle in for the night I lit the candle that was stationary on the wall by the door, I in turn laid down beside him looking at what was on the television, after a while I drifted off to sleep forgetting the candle was lit. The next thing I knew I felt a deep bump on the bed, as I was awaken by this feeling, the next thing I saw was flames, nothing but flames, and he was fighting the fire trying to put it out **(Mercy God!)** with clothing around his hand, remember he was drunk to the point he could not stand up straight, somehow he was able to put out the flames that were by the door, the only way out **(please allow me to take a moment here to breathe Whooo!)** just thinking about it again just takes, my breath way **(BUT GOD!).** God is a protector and keeper of life. **Psalm 27: 5 for in times of trouble he shall hide me in his pavilion: in the secret of His tabernacle shall he hide me: he shall set me upon a rock.**

This could have been my last day on this earth, But God seen that it was good for me to stay here to share this and encourage someone with my life testimony. I was so afraid it shook me up for a whole month. Eventually we broke up over this, we stayed a part for a month but we got back together. I tried to hold on to our relationship but his drinking was the biggest of our problems and being as young as I was I didn't know how to handle this. He uses to get drunk and lay out on our porch my mother liked him because he was a respectable man to her but the drinking did not set well with her. Mother allowed him to hang out at our house just to keep an eye on our relationship but I eventually I let him go. On the fire incident God kept me from death again at the age of seventeen.

Daniel 6: 19 20 21 22 Then the king arose very early in the morning, and went in haste in unto the den of lions. And when he come to the den, he cried with a lamentable voice unto Daniel: and the king spake and said to Daniel, O Daniel, servant of the living God, is thy God, whom thou Servest continually, able to deliver thee from the lions? Then said Daniel unto the king O king, live forever. My God hath sent his angel, and hath shut the lions' mouths, that they have not hurt me: forasmuch as before him innocence was found in me; and also before thee, O king, have I done no hurt.

Daniel 3: 22 23 25 Therefore because the King's commandment was urgent, and the furnace exceeding hot. The flame of the fire slew those men that took up Sha'-drach,

Me'-shach, and A-bed-ne-go. And these three men, Sha'-drach, Me'-shach, and A-bed-ne-go fell down bound into the midst of the burning fiery furnace.

Then Neb-u-chad- nez'-zar the king was astoined, and rose up in haste, and spake, and said unto his counselors, Did not we cast three men bound into the midst of the fire? They answered and said unto the king, True, O king. He answered and said, Lo, I see four men loose, walking in the midst of the fire, and they have no hurt; and the form of the fourth is like the Son of God.

THE GUN

Here I stand with another accident in my life that I could have been gone, **(BUT GOD!).** I was working for Churches Chicken a fast food restaurant in Washington DC. I was standing at my cash register taking my daily morning orders. A man came in to order, he did order, but at the same time he pulled out a gun stuck it in my face with the trigger pull back. All I could see at that moment was the opening of his barrel a big black round whole staring at me. Whooo! Then I **heard ("B.......")** give me the money. At that moment the only thing I had to do is to push one little button on the cash register and the draw automatically opens, he leaned over the counter and took out what was in the draw. I could have gotten killed over $57 dollars, that day I had counted my draw before the store open and that's all I had to start with. God's love and kindness, mercy, and grace that keeps the enemy's hand from doing what he wants to do.

We do not have control over what happens but God is our creator and life sustainer.

Psalms 27: 1 The Lord is my light and my salvation who shall I fear? The Lord is the strength of my life; of whom shall I be afraid.

There was another occasion I was working for the same company but in another location. I was working the drive thru at this store, my back was away from the inside area of the store I was waiting on a drive thru customer, suddenly I heard a thumping sound I turn to see what it was (mercy!) this guy had jump over the counter wearing a black mask over his face carrying a semi automatic hand gun. He pointed that gun right in my face telling everybody to stand still and don't move **(WOW!)** Gods' angels just keep on shielding me **Hallelujah!** There were other guys with him that day they robbed us for a couple of thousand. **(Psalm 23: 4) Yea though I walk through the valley of the shadow of death, I will fear no evil: for thou art with me; thy rod and staff they comfort me.** I say keep your trust in God he will see you through.

CHAPTER FIVE

I Must Inspire You To Stand In God And Have Faith

I'm praying, as you read this book you will be inspired about what has been written, by the mercy and goodness of our Lord Jesus Christ, the Father, and the Holy Spirit that which is in heaven. Jesus Christ paid a price that my life cannot compare, his blood wipe away the iniquity of my life. Some of the incident had been bad choices, that I made on my own and his body that was torn for all the issues I had to endure. As we continue on this journey of life we will endure a lot of hardships, God is our deliverer of them all. By this time I know the thought pattern is, is there more, yes my friends there is more to come, all has not been bad, this is just small

Highlights how God has seen me through. If you find yourself in one of these life situation s and you think your not going to make it hold on, God is at the door there is a route of escape, keep your eyes on Him, stand still see the salvation of God and the power of the Lord. It is His holy power that is allowing you to read this book. It's not over yet, until God say's it over, remember that old saying **("it's not over until the fat lady sing,")** God is that fat lady He starts singing but it's not over until he has finished the song, Ha! Ha! Ha! Hallelujah! Yea and Amen, the only way to stay strong is to study. **II Timothy 2: 15 Study to show thyself approved unto God a workman that needed not to be ashamed, rightly dividing the word of truth. Romans 12:2 And be not conformed to this world but be ye transformed by the renewing of your mind that ye may prove what is that good and acceptable and perfect, well of God. Luck 12: 48 But he that knew not, and did commit things worthy of stripes, shall be beaten with little stripe. For unto whomsoever much is given, of him shall be much required: and to whom men have committed much, of him they will ask the more.** God gives us life and it is required of us to live with him in our lives.

CHAPTER SIX

The Chip Tooth, The Torn Flesh

As a child life was testing I haven't mention everything just the life experiences that I believe without God I couldn't have made it from family problems to boys to men problems, fighting in school to the neighborhood brawls. One time while I was attending Jr. High School I was in the hall way standing in line with my class mates to attend assembly in the auditorium at this particular time this boy in my class had got himself in some trouble and it was said that I was the one who had told on him. It wasn't me; however this person believed what he heard and he walk up to me in the line and punch me right in the mouth with his fist it broke one of my front bottom teeth causing much pain the tooth had chip to the nerve. My mother took me to the dentist he patch my tooth with a sealing cement that covered it so the nerve wouldn't be exposed. To this day the tooth is still chipped the good thing is that there is no pain. Sit back and think for a moment, our spiritual lives are similar to that tooth of mind. The enemy accuses us of something every day. The word of God states that he is the accuser of the brethren. The enemy uses those who are weak in spirit, and them that do not accept God as their personal savior accuses us and gives us a punch in our spirit that will break into our spiritual nerve that will cause much pain. When this happens just allow God to mend it with his anointed plaster cement, that's his Holy power to cover that so you can go on and live with no pain. God loves us so much he will patch up our wounds so we can continue to do his will, it's all about him and not about us. While sitting here at my computer listening to some good Godly music that moves my soul, I must mention the time when my middle finger was torn open by the school door.

I was in the girls' choir and the boys were playing at the class door and I was trying to stop them by pushing the door open. One of the boys gave that big old door a punch and my finger got caught in it and my middle finger got torn open where you could see the bone. The doctors had to repair the torn ligament so my finger would have normal movement I would be able to straighten it out and bend it. This reminds me of the wounds that Jesus bore, and the scars for which he had bared for us, the flesh was hanging off his body. Just imagine this for a moment my little finger took on its own small trauma, but Jesus took on a big trauma for us he was crucified for our sins and bruised for our transgressions. **Matthew 27:25-66 Mark 15**

HEART PROBLEMS

As I continue I remember other things started to happen, my mother and the man I call daddy began to fight. Let me back up just for a minute before I continue, as a child fighting through the pneumonia stage, I had a heart murmur, my heart had an irregular heart beat my heart would skip a beat that would cause me to have shortness of breath and become very tired. I don't know if it was cause by the pneumonia or I was just born with it. As I attended Jr. High School my breathing would sometimes become irregular making it hard for me to breathe. My mother noticed when I would take a deep breath it looked as if I was having trouble breathing. She asked me what was wrong I said it feels like I can't breathe she took me to children's hospital at DC General the doctor kept me for a few days they put me on a walking machine and a breathing tube while I was walking and had a EKG performed after each exercise and then one was done while I was resting.

The findings were as I began to exercise my heart would beat on a normal rhythm and my breathing became normal but while I was resting my heart would start skipping a irregular rhythm the atrium opening was not opening up in between rhythms that cause the blood not to flow through properly causing my oxygen level to become low in my lungs. As I exercised my heart started to beat on a normal rhythm. The doctor's conclusion was I didn't need to be put on medication for this problem the only thing they said I needed was plenty of exercise, this would straighten my heart. I was interested in running track for the school track team, the prescription was just what I needed exercise. **(Humm! Isn't that something?)** The outcome is that I did run track for the school track team and everything turn out all right even thou the heart murmur was still there, the heart is the life line for the human body it cannot operate without it; the heart is where God speaks. **John 14:1 Let not your heart be trouble ye believe in God believe also in me** This is where he wants us to be in him, with this book he has inspired me to write it will help us to draw closer to him in his kingdom. Even now I can say I'm writing under God's anointing with the guidance of the Holy Spirit who brings all things back to my remembrance. **John 14: 26 but the** comforter, which is the Holy Ghost, whom the Father will send in my name, he shall teach you all things, and bring all things to your remembrance, what so ever I have said unto you.

CHAPTER SEVEN

Living Through The Fights

Living through the fights my parents started fighting during my early teen years. Remembering my parent's fights began to come more often on the weekends during the house parties. After each party mother and my stepfather would somehow start a Conversation about the past and they would start to fight. These fights would last all night up into morning. One night I heard them fighting what I mean by fighting they where physical with blood spots on the floor I would hear them breaking glass, bumping and cursing these fights started happening for what I can remember about the age of thirteen. I can remember hearing these disturbing noises while I was in my bed. My heart felt like it would stop and my stomach would begin to knot up I started to talk to God we call it prayer. I can recall saying my pray **Lord Please God! Don't let nothing bad happen to my mother or father they are fighting help God.** With tears running down my face I would do this until I went to sleep I would awake the next morning with the house torn apart in shambles broken liquor glasses and beer cans. I would find mother on the couch sleep with a hangover, my stepfather would not be home where he was I didn't know.

I would just start to clean the house until my mother's awake, I thank God through all of those fights everything would turned out all right God spared them both through these storms. I do believe God taught me how to pray I believe this was purpose to make me who I am today.

I 'm a prayer Warrior for the Lord he alerts me when I need to pray when something is not right or someone who is in trouble, I will get this unsettling feeling within my spirit man until I lay on my face before God and lay in his presence, he calms my spirit and by his anointing power will reveal the persons or a thing I should pray about.

If you are in this situation while reading this book allow me to encourage your heart, God is shaping you in the midst of it all; it seems hard now but hold fast to God and pray, believe that God is going to make it alright.

Jeremiah 18:3-6 Then I went down to the potter's house and behold he wrought a work and the wheels and the vessel that he made of clay was marred in the hand of the potter so he made it again another vessel, as seemed good to the potter to make it. and the word of the Lord came to me saying o house of Israel cannot I do with you as this potter saith the Lord behold as the clay is in the potter's hand, so are ye in mine hand O house of Israel (ALLOW GOD TO SHAPE YOU IN YOUR STORM)

YOU ARE TOO YOUNG TO SERVE GOD

In my heart I always was close to God even while I was in sin. One summer I was in North Carolina on my summer break from school there was a lady that lived in the projects where my mother's oldest sister lived. This lady was as some people would call her a very religious Christian, she used to call the children in the neighborhood to her porch and she would read the bible to us and then she would take us in her house and told us to get down on our needs to pray asking God to forgive us of our sins I took it personal and hold it to my heart, I knew there was a change immediately and I was looking forward to this new life I had just said yes to. The summer was over I went home to my mother I told my mother what had happen and I was not ready for the response I received from her, my grandmother being a preacher and all, I thought my mother would be happy for me and guide me but instead she stood in the kitchen and said Beverly you don't know what you are doing, you are still young and you must live your young life, and continue doing things that young girls do.

You would be depriving yourself of what you as a young girl love to do boys, movies, parties, I stood by her side saying nothing back my mind started thinking about what my mother had said and my heart dropped I just said ok and walk out of the kitchen. I didn't give it another thought I just started doing the things I always did. As I mentioned earlier in chapter two all of those things started happening I know what you are thinking right about now if you are a Christian reading this portion of my life you must be saying **(What!)** that is not right; however if you are not yet in the fold of Christ and say's it ok allow me as an forty-six year old Evangelist to inform you of what **(Proverb 22: 6)** say's **"Train up a child in the way he should go: and when he is old, he will not depart from it", (Matthew 19:14 -15) Jesus said, suffer the little children, and forbid them not, to come unto me: for of such is the kingdom of heaven. And he laid his hands on them, and departed thence).** This book is to help encourage someone to come into God's kingdom. My mother felt she was doing a good thing, she was not in Christ she allowed Satan to coach her telling me not to live for Christ because he knew what God plans were for my life, and Satan had a plan to work his wicked devices to destroy my life mentally, emotionally, physically. Satan did not want me to live pass the ninth month of life **(BUT GOD!)** You see God had put His hand upon me and marked me for His Glory. That's why he awaken me in the mid day as I was resting God spoke to me and saying, Beverly you are going to write a book, **(what book)!** in my thought pattern thinking I'm not a good writer, my spelling is off, my grammar is bad who wants to hear what I have to say any way. God heard I and he said to me your life testimony but only a few high lights of how I brought you through them with my word attached.

Now here it is I pray this book well help inspire, and up lift someone in some way through the love of Christ with his holy anointing power to draw his people into himself where he wants them to be in him. This is a tool he has given me to use to help draw his people into his kingdom. I am writing this book under the anointing of God. God's holy spirit brings all things back to my remembrance **(John 14: 26) But the Comforter, which is the Holy Ghost, whom the Father will send in my name, he shall teach you all things, and bring all things to your remembrance, whatsoever I have said unto you.**

THINGS BEGAN TO CHANGE

Things began to change, I noticed something about myself, when I prayed and asked God for something it happened, I didn't ask for a lot I just asked God for a little sister I was the only child for a long time when I did not want to play with the children in the neighborhood I stayed in the house. My mother used to urge me to go out and not hang around the house too much. She said it was good to go out and play with the other children. But I liked the inside better so I wanted to have someone to play with while I was inside where we lived. I prayed for a long time for my sister to come forth then one day my mother came to me and said Beverly I want to ask you a question she said, how you would feel if I had another child. My heart started to beat with excitement then I said yes! My mother said to me I have something to tell you, what I said **(what)!** You are going to have a **(baby)!** She said yes, I'm Pregnant **(Good God O mighty)!** Look at God just thinking about how God works is amazing. So she had my little sister, she is not so little any more, she has been my joy, and she is my inspiration every since she first arrived on the scene I was twelve years old.

My mother was surprise herself she didn't think she could bring forth anymore children because she had only one good fallopian tube because my biological father he had caused her to contract a sexually transmitted disease that limited her to bare children for twelve years. My sister is a very special woman of God; you see she started taken steps and walking at the age of five months, yes! I said five months **(how?)** we have yet to understand, God does tell us that his ways are not our ways, and his thoughts are not our thoughts. She is not just a miracle baby but she had the ability to walk at an early age that normally Other babies could not have done at this age. I know this book is suppose to be me; however it is about me I'm just mentioning how God works miracles with people that he has given to me as a family. Now she is dancing for the Lord, she is an account assistant she was skipped in high school from algebra one to intermitted algebra this girl is bless. On another occasion I prayed to God asking him for a child because I didn't believe I was good enough to become some man's wife I had relationship after relationship but just couldn't seem to keep one so I ask God to bless me with a child. It is understandable that I was supposed to be married, but that just did not happen for me right away, when it did happen it didn't last long. I joined the military and met this guy, we started dating and time moved on we were growing deeper involved with each other his father wanted us to marry but that didn't happen. He had a love for the street life and he had a fantasy about being a pimp, we went through ups and downs in and out of our relationship, during the high times of our relationship I became pregnant with my daughter, God created another miracle in my life, she is my rose from God's heaven.

God had this purposed right from the start; she was eighteen when her father had his share of life ups and downs by this time we were not together any more. God had another purpose planned for my life, and he was not getting it together so I had to move on. But the miracle of her life is that her father needed a kidney and he only had one more year to receive a good kidney. Our daughter, my Warrior, my Rose, and my friend answered the call to give her father her kidney, I believe this is the reason God allowed me to bring her forth. Our daughter gave her father one of her kidney in June 2004. The doctors found an unusual discovery she had two extra veins to each kidneys, her doctor told me that this is very rare and he himself only performed surgery on two people before her and she is two out of a thousand people that has this type of kidney, God knows how to do it right, they where a match and he is doing well with his new kidney. I asked the doctor about the two extra veins she has after the kidney was remove he said he tied them all together and pushes them to the side. I do believe with another miracle God can replace her kidney with a new one that is why he gave her two extra veins along with the two she already has. You only need two for each kidney to live. God answer another prayer and she came with a big purpose. She is doing well and living her life to the fullest. God didn't stop there he gave me a son also he has favor as the book of proverbs say's he is my preacher he has acting ability, he knows how to persuade people to see it his way, God will come through in his own time not in ours. **Matthew 7:7 ask and it shall be given to you seek and ye shall find knock and it shall be opened unto you. I John 5:14-15 and this is the confidence that we have in him, that, if we ask any thing according to his will, he heareth us: And if we know that he hear us, whatsoever we ask, we know that we have petitions that we desired of him.**

CHAPTER EIGHT

Life Is Moving On

As life moves on I joined the military while I was still in high school, I was placed on the split option program, this program allowed high school students to join the military while they are still in school, as long as you join doing your senior year for the summer. After basic training I was sent to Quarter Master training school to be trained in the job I was going to perform while serving in the military. While I was at school in Fort Lee Virginia, I met a handsome young man he looked to be settle, but there was something about him that was not revealed until later in our relationship. As we dated at Fort Lee where we met, we grew closer to each other, the time came that we had to part so we kept our relationship going. Eventually it became a long distance relationship and after high school graduation I started traveling to see him as often as I could and he did the same. Time is moving on, he asks me to come to Ohio to live so we could be near each other. By this time my mother was having her last child, she had remarried for the third time she was starting a new family. So I informed her about my decision t move to Ohio. She didn't like it of course she wanted me to stay with her to help with the girls. Being a young woman I wanted my own family I looked at this opportunity to get away and learn life on my own. Our relationship grew apart because of my decision to leave home. By having a new friend in life, I was banking on our relationship to grow into marriage I always wanted to be married. I did not leave for Ohio right away I dated him, visited him off and on for a whole year getting to know his family and they getting to know me everything was working out so I moved there.

He was the last child in his family he had two older sisters they liked me very much. As time went on we settled together living with his parents, I didn't know what I was doing living with him and his parents, please somebody **(Slap me LOL!)** my eyes were blinded by the mere fact of having someone to love me, we didn't know what love was all about we had sex and it felt good we thought that was it **(NO!)** its more to it then sex my friends. We started having problems remember the secret that he had well, it eventually showed up in our relationship he started going out with other girls, (sound familiar) he wanted to be a pimp, he was fascinated with street life. By the early 80's the pimp life was booming big so he wanted this kind of life and everything that came with it girls, drugs, and money fortunately that wasn't my way of living my family didn't bring me up to live that way and his parent didn't either. He had a lot of girls some of them the family knew them well but his mother didn't allow them at the house. This didn't bother me as long I could be with him, he call me his main woman the fantasy was him having a woman at home while having girls in the street. I went along with this because my heart was so caught up in him nothing else mattered. I thank my God I wasn't the type to run the streets I always had a settled mind, family was in the plan although I was with the wrong person. Time went on I didn't understand why he had to be in the street with those girls knowing I was there for him. There were a side of him that was clean, but he had this fantasy that over ride his feelings for me. So he became the pimp, this left me feeling unwanted at times, he would tell me that he loved me and he call me his wife to keep me with him I found it to be alright at that time.

You supposed to stay home and be here when I come home that's why you are here, my parents allow you to stay here for me I believed that lie. Remember my mother went through a similar situation with my biological father.

I accepted it because I wanted to be with him. I didn't know too much about street life other than what I heard from people I knew. Unfortunately he love the street more than he loved me. Time continue to move on we had a daughter together after the birth of our little girl we broke up. His parents allowed me to stay their because of the baby but we slept in separate bedrooms, eventually I moved out of the house and got my own place in Ohio. It was an adventure that would never be forgotten, we went back and forth with our relationship for a long time. When our daughter was born he was hoping for a boy he was with me every step of the way until after the birth of our daughter because of our first born wasn't a boy he started ignoring his responsibility he gave me a hard time about being the father he said he would be. He left his responsibility on his family, his parents took over all the financial responsibility of our daughter, from buying food, pampers, and all the other necessities that she needed by being a baby it help out a lot along with what I was doing as a young mother I had my daughter at the age of twenty-one. He stood in front of me after we brought her home from the hospital just before Christmas and said we do not have anything else to do with each other Bev other than our daughter we are through that cut me hard my understanding didn't come, my heart dropped we had been in this relationship about three years and just like that it's over. I couldn't believe this was happening to me; we never had any argument or fights. Our baby girl was born on December 18, 1984 she was suppose to be born on his Birthday which is December 15th. I allowed this to happen hoping to become his wife one day, it was hard letting go I thought I have found my one and only love, to have a family with but not so in this case. Because of his love for the street yes he had his life he wanted, but now that life is over, the years as of this day he is locked up for drug trafficking.

Our daughter is a grown woman now and she is still more beautiful than ever. God gave her to us for a blessing; this blessing came in the form of life giving. Over a period of time in the past he got hurt and needed a kidney, he had only one more year to be on list for a kidney transplant but the hospital didn't have one for him, **(But God!)** our daughter, the one he neglected until she was thirteen she was the one who held his life stored inside her, God allowed her to have two extra veins that connected to each kidney; God already knew she was the one to save his life. Our daughter come to a decision to give her dad one of her kidneys when she turned eighteen we had talked about it when she was about thirteen and she did. God always knew what he was doing. **WE SET OUR**

LIFE IN ONE DIRECTION THAT CAN LEAD TO DESTRUCTION BUT GOD HAS ANOTHER ROAD THAT IS A ROAD OF LIFE, GOD HAS A PLAN THAT WE CAN NOT SEE, THERE COULD BE A PERSON YOU FEEL THAT YOU MAY NOT LIKE OR EVEN DON'T THINK OF OFTEN. REMEMBER THAT PERSON MAY BE HOLDING YOUR LIFE IN HIS OR HER HANDS, THAT PERSON MAY BE WHO GOD USES TO SAVE YOUR LIFE.

1John 3: 17- 18 But whoso hath this world's good, and seeth his brother have need, and shutteth up his bowels of compassion form him, how dwelleth the love of God in him? My Little children let us not love in word, neither in tongue; but in deed and in truth

CHAPTER NINE

Becoming A Christian

In the year 1986 two years after my daughter was born I found myself alone again her father and I parted for good. I stayed in Ohio for a while I became depress and seeing shadows moving in my home. I called my auntie who lives in North Carolina she explained to me what was happening to me she, said to me during our phone conversation the Lord is trying to get your attention honey do you know you are marked for Christ and Satan wants to destroy your life you must surrender your life to God. At this point I didn't know what to do I just knew I couldn't go on being in this state of mind. She said to me are you ready to say yes to God Beverly, I said yes then I surrendered right then, she read **(Romans 10: 9)** to me and it say's " **If thy shall confess the Lord Jesus Christ with thy mouth and believe in thy heart God has raised him from the dead thou shall be save."** Meaning Jesus. Tears just fell from my eyes and I just cried and cried sobbing before God after she had prayed with me and for me she seal it with this prayer in the Name of our Lord Jesus Christ let it be known in heaven that you are saved, I had to repeat that to her then she said girl you now in the kingdom of God you must find a church where you can grow in the Lord because now you have to fight Satan until Jesus comes back. She is one of my mother's sisters that I was very close to she took me to be her own, I could talk to her about anything things I couldn't talk to my mother about, my life was placed in her hands and she took that advantage to lead me to Christ and save my life and help me to be a soldier for God. I found a church a friend of mine whom I went to beauty school with I told her what had happen and she instantly invited me to her church to visit, I did just that and my Christian journey began.

Not only did I join, God baptized me with his Holy Spirit, his non quenching fire, and his electricity of power with the gift of unknown tongue. An experience I will never ever forget as long as I live, God then demonstrated to me his mighty power through me to deliver one of my family members out of the bondage of Satan's grip. **(OUR GOD IS AN AWESOME GOD!)** Being a new babe in the Lord, God took the liberty to teach me his mighty power **(WOW!)** this demonic spirit was cast out by the almighty God himself through me. Nobody else knew the school I was in learning under the mighty hand of God with no other man's help as a young Christian. In my life as a Christian things happen, words cannot describe in this chapter. I'm just highlighting the awesomeness of God's power in my life. Being in a Christian marriage was a must so I started praying for God to send me a husband, **(Oh!)** yes the husband came he was one of the Elite Elders in the church we attended. Unfortunately, this was not what God wanted for me; sometimes people can pressure you to move out of the will of God in the name of religion. I say stand fast, pray, seek God, and wait until you get a real answer from him, no matter how long it takes God has a good and perfect gift for you if you just wait. **Isaiah 55: 8, 9 For my thought are not your thoughts, neither are your ways my ways, saith the Lord. For as the heavens are higher than the earth, so are my ways higher than your ways, and my thoughts than your thoughts.** Our marriage only lasted eleven and half months my so call bible totting theologian teacher supposed to have been a man of God, church elder he had so much going on wrong that I had to get out of that so call marriage of ours, because of the life he lived outside of the church, this life would have cost me my life **(But God!)** his awesome mercy for me and a purpose for my life. Satan had a hidden agenda for me I couldn't see because I was not strong in God's word to see I just knew I needed a husband for religion sake. He was a bible totting, bisexual preacher and was hooked up with the town mafia **(WAIT!)** GOD saved me from that destruction **Hallelujah!** After this I came back home here to the metropolitan area. I met my son's biological father we were supposed to be just friends but our friendship didn't last long was just getting out of a bad marriage it was taking a toll on me and I gave into the pleasures of my flesh. What came from that was a beautiful and handsome baby boy who God has ordained to preach his gospel (he just don't know it yet) one day. My daughter's father has the same name as his father but the difference is my son's father is a minister of God's gospel. To this day I do not know where he is **(God just knows how to do it right!)** This didn't stop my walk with God it was embarrassing, and taunting Satan used my family a lot to try to break me and lash out at me, my family and I weren't as close as we are now to God be the glory. Satan use them a lot to lash out at me. But I stood that test it was painful I had to go through that and it wasn't easy at all heart ache, tears and prayers a lot of praying, my mother was not a Christian she only went to church when she thought she needed to go. She knew about God because of her mother, my mother lived her life just the opposite of how her mother taught her. The good news is right now to this very day my mother is giving God all she got she is a deaconess in the church where she and my sister attend. I had problems with my family in the past it was not easy **(But God!)** my mother and I could not sit down with each other and talk about the goodness of the Lord she allowed me to anoint her when she had surgery. I remember the day she didn't even want to hear anything I had to say about God, **(WOW! Look at God)** what a mighty God we serve, prayer changes all things in due time.

My daughter's father was there even though we didn't make a home with each other we remain friends after the hurt was gone he accepted my son to be his. He would send clothing and money for the both of them, to this day my son only knows him as his father. Yes he continues to live that life he loves so much and because of that life he chose, he is still locked up serving time. But thank God he is alive and well. Being a Christian didn't excuse me from doing the things that were not good in God's sight. But the grace of my father who is in heaven allows me to stay here to try to get it right. We all fall short sometimes but we must get it right get back up and do it again. I have had my in and out relationships hoping that someone would find me special they didn't because I had to see myself special first before anyone else could see me special. It didn't come until later on in my walk with Christ but all the time God was perfecting me for the ministry, working some stuff out of me.

DELIVERANCE HAS COME

I found myself back in Ohio after my second marriage to an old friend. I didn't obey God I knew that this was not going to work out but I was afraid of being by myself so I said yes for the second time this time no body rushed me but me. In this marriage I was still hurting from the pain my daughter's father has cause and my first husband; my grandmother passed away talk about hurt. Unpleasant things started to happen in this marriage he stared being abusive telling me I wasn't good enough for him that the women he had before me were better after we had intimacy bed time, then the fight would start, he would call the pastor about our bed life and everyone who he could talk to in the church. Our private home life was out around the church I found my way out.

I was stress to the point I couldn't take it anymore. I took drastic measures, one night I drew a knife on him dare him to move. My thought pattern was off I only seen blood dripping from my sight **(But God!)** I heard my daughter crying out then I turn to see what was wrong she was standing at the door saying mommy no! Please no! Everything that was not like God seem to leave me, my thought pattern returned and I was able to think clearly, that's when I made the decision to let go and move on. I fell down on my knees after that night. We had broken up God spoke to me you have disobey me again the first time you didn't know but this time you knew.

Luke 12:47, 48 and that servant which knew his Lord's will, and prepared not himself, neither I according to his will, shall be beaten with many stripes. But he that knew not and I commit things worthy of stripes shall be beaten with few stripes. Fore unto whomsoever much is given, of him shall be much required and to who men have committed much, of him they will ask the more. With the same anointing he had place on me, when he baptized me with his holy power is the same way he took it back. I felt the virtue leave the same way it fell on me, from that moment on I was in a back sliding state I wondered in my wilderness for about a year or two, my daughter's father had gotten hurt they didn't expect for him to live through the night, after he returned home from the hospital I went back to Ohio to help his mother with him hoping this time we could make things work. God came through for him allowed him to stay here to get things right but instead he went back to the street life doing the same thing. I found me apartment with the children I started smoking, having sex with whatever guy I met thinking I was having a real relationship that was not it, God allowed me to go through this for a Chastisement and to bring me back to a repentant heart.

As time moved on I was puffing away on those cigarettes smoking about two packs a day. But I thank my God he didn't allow me to get into drugs my demons were smoking cigarettes and sex, every time I met a new guy friend I just had to try him out it made me feel good inside so I thought. One day a notion came over me to go back to school to try to make it for me and my children what I didn't know was God was setting me up for deliverance, the college I attended the recruiter asked me if I was in a church I told him, no I stop going to church for a while he ask me to visit his church that was on the other side of where I lived I took the information. I started school and eventually I did visit his church, after that, things started happening where I had to stop school and go back to work, the children and I started going to his church, I joined and God guided me to a conference, that the church had. It was set up at a hotel that Sunday my life changed during the conference, the conference was teaching on the purpose of a thing and the church it was taught by Dr. Miles Monroe his teaching touched me from the depth of my soul I held on to every word after that conference. Something began to happen to me I went back into that depress state I was in before giving my life to Christ, but this time I didn't have anybody to call on, it was me and God I had gotten so depress this time around that it had gotten hard for me to function for work and to even deal with the children, a friend of mine would come over and take the children for the weekend for me we took turns having each other children on alternate weekends she wasn't a church going person but she said she knew God. At this particular time I had asked her to come over to get the children early for me.

God led me to open my bible and to study what I had received from the conference while I was studying, God led me to open the book of **(Revelation 4: 1-4)** by the time I finished the third verse it seems like the words just jump right off the page of my bible and those words went inside of me, at this time I started to cry and sobbing before God, everything in my house appeared to be spinning around I started having visions of my first husband with his woman in the bars, the voice of my second husband telling me I wasn't good enough for him, my mother telling me she wish she would had given me away when other family members ask to have me, all of that kept me crying out to God please help me, God please help me, for three days and nights.

I found myself on my living room floor ball up in a fetal position sweat was pouring off of me, like a women in hot flashes, I threw up a couple of times. Every time each vision or a voice would come back I remember crying out

God! Make it stop please God! Then calmness came over me and a voice said to me to pray in the unknown tongue I had received the day I gave my life to Christ I did it. When I opened my mouth and I started speaking another language I didn't know of and I had no understanding at the time, I just did it and this kept on happening for a couple of hours. I couldn't stop myself from speaking this unknown language. Afterward my mouth stopped and a calmness came over me again I just laid there on the floor all by myself until I could get up. My eyes opened and at this time I heard a voice saying I am your God! I have driven all of your demons away; no man will get the glory of you deliverance.

This day you are delivered go smoke no more and wait on my voice to tell you of the instructions for everything, then the voice said Beverly I am your God of whom you have read in the book of Revelation. I looked like the stone and if I look like the stones so do you go and know your purpose I have given you. After this I didn't know how to tell anybody what had happen to me by the time the children came back home that Monday I was ready to do what I had to do for my family remembering no more of my past until this day as I write this book.

II Timothy 4:17-18 Not with standing the Lord stood with me and strengthened me that by me the preaching might be fully known, and that all the Gentiles might

hear: and I was delivered out of the mouth of the lion. And the Lord shall deliver me from every evil work, and will preserve me unto his heavenly kingdom to who be glory forever and ever Amen.

CHAPTER TEN

Homeless And Confused

Being a mother with two children and living for Christ God had been and still is my refuge. I raised my children without a husband, an earthy one I'm talking about. The children and I always prayed together we dance and learn God's way of living. Being a single parent I had to rely on God to teach me how to take care of my children it was scary. We left Cincinnati after my awesome deliverance, my mother was asking me to come back to stay with her so she can help me with the children so we moved back with my family here in the metropolitan area.

I stayed with them for a while until my family and I

started going through personality conflicts and spiritual struggles, for some reason my mother and I didn't see things the same way this started a lot of confusion, things where said that hurt and my mother ask me to leave her house, because of this I found myself homeless for a few days my family drove me around DC to try to found a shelter to put me in but not one was open. I was dropped off at my friend s house around where my mother lived, he asks me what had happened and I told him the story. He said he could not let me stay with him because he was leaving in the morning he was in the military and was going a way for a week; he introduced me to his cousin he ask them to let me stay with them until he return. He said to me if you are still with my family when I return then you can stay with me at this time I was desperate. So they put us up in their empty room for a few days and we sleep on the floor until my aunt found where we were.

The children and I lived with my aunt for a year and a half while I was living with her and my uncle their house had four room, her oldest daughter was still home with them so we share the same room, with her and her three small children. Our children slept in the fourth room next to ours.

Brokenness

My spirit was broken because of the things my mother had said to me that I really didn't think she would ever say, and I had said something back to her in anger, I was so hurt and broken my stomach was upset I could have thrown up, my heart hurt so bad because my mother and I had a good relationship until her third marriage, me leaving for Ohio. My Aunt's love for her family helped me to deal with the brokenness and anger; she would come in our room in the morning at 4:00A.M. wake me she would order me yes, she ordered me to get up and pray with her in the children's room, she taught me how to stretch out on my face before God, we cried together and she would pray until her spirit would feel better for that day, some days she would be late getting to work for me. This continued for a while and then she got a break through with me, I shared with her what God had given me. God had spoken to my spirit while sleeping and told me to open my word and read, **Psalm 51: 10-17 create in me a clean heart, O God; and renew a right spirit within me. Cast me not away from thy presence; and take not thy holy spirit from me. Restore unto me the Joy of thy salvation; and uphold me with thy free spirit. Then will I teach transgressors thy ways; and sinners shall be converted unto thee.**

Deliver me from blood guiltiness, O God thou God

of my salvation; and my tongue shall sing aloud of thy righteousness.

O Lord, open thou my lips; and my mouth shall show forth thy praise. For thou desires not sacrifice; else would I give it: thou delights not in burnt offering. The sacrifices of God are a broken spirit; a broken and a contrite heart, O God thou wilt not despise. As I was reading this each day, each week, and months my heart was healing and mending. I got myself together and started looking for a job and apartment for me and my children. I also went back to school God had opened that door for me the State paid for it so I took up a new trade. From this point on I continually to serve God took my children to church prayed with them I was doing Ok.

Being the other woman

I started working again, I worked part time at the hospital that's when I met a handsome down to earth guy he worked there also as a police officer. He would ask about me, and he would stop me in the hall to talk. So we stated talking I informed him that I was not interested because he was married, he kept on pursuing me and he was not about to give up his chase, I liked him as well but I didn't want to get involved with him because he was married; however as we continued to see each other in the hall I would ask different personal question, he wouldn't lie to me he just kept trying to persuade me telling me we could be just friends. **"If that wasn't the biggest lie that sound like the truth, for if I never heard it before"** but it sound ok to me at the time. I kept on seeing him we got deeper involved with each other, then sex came into play after a year, then I introduced him to my children I finally gave into the relationship. He was good for us, helping us with a lot of things, by working part time and on state funds I didn't mine the help the extra cash came in handy.

I dated him for seven years we went out for lunch, he came over for dinner three times a week and sex, I visited him at work doing what a wife does but I was not one **Ha!** At the time I didn't care about being married because I had two failed one and just didn't care to get married again or didn't I feel that any man wanted me for a real wife. My first husband the Elder in our church he stayed in the streets I was only 25years old and he was 42 I thought I had found something thinking that because he was older not so. My second marriage we just did make it so at this point of my life I said I'll play it safe but it was not right in the eyes of God I had a low self esteem thinking I was ok. Yes, I was a Christian and in this kind of relationship that I was praying for it to lead into marriage that's how deep I had gone with him. For six years everything was good until I joined the military to help with food that small amount kept me going because by this time I was working full time and welfare had cut me off he helped with the difference. It came to a point I had to be deployed to serve in the Iran war in2003-2004 at Fort Dix New Jersey, we stayed in touch with each other by phone he called me twice a day and night sometimes three times a week, before I go on let me back up, I gave him my furniture he stated he was leaving his wife and he had gotten an apartment, I help him furnish the apartment so I gave him my furniture because I did not want to pay for storage and I was going to be gone for a year. The apartment was a place where, I came to when I came home on leave my children were with my mother while I was serving in the military, a lot of people were angry with me and I didn't even know it. This was a move I decided make so I could keep my family fed.

He was angry and didn't allow me to know it so he started another relationship while I was a way with other women. Not only that he was still staying at the house where he and his wife lived, I would ask him why he was still there he would just say he had to pay his portion of the house it was a court order so he feels that as long as he had to pay he was not going to leave his house. He rented the apartment to his friends for sex nights and gave his wife a key to the apartment, I saw them coming out one night when I went there to see if he was home, and to see what was going on. He lied to me about a lot of things I try to hold on to someone who was never mine. God allowed all these things to come to past for my good.

Romans 8: 28 And we know that all things work together for good to them that love God, to them who are the called according to his purpose. While coming home on leave I wanted to stay at the apartment I call him thinking he was at work. He told me the apartment was there for me to stay in with him while on leave. He always knew when I arrived, but this time he didn't answer his phone for a while he had me waiting about an hour after I had arrived.

When he arrived at the apartment he was angry and he started fussing with me about calling him he had his uniform on as if he was working I remembered this was an off night and it was, I didn't allow myself to fuss back something deep inside of me knew things were just about over with us; But still I try to hold on he just fussed and fussed then the question was ask, about his wife with the key he told me she only has the key to the front door to the apartment building, he said to me don't you worry about my wife. He started pointing his finger in my face and said you think everything should stop when you come home, and I'm supposed to be here with you every time.

You can stay here but me 'm not going to be here with you there are other things I'm doing. This was so disappointing to me and there was sadness and I felt belittled because we had never had a fight, nor fussed to this multitude, he just changed right in front of my eyes then it was revealed to me he was seeing someone else. Never allowed myself to open all the way with him because, there was always a possibility that he would stay with his wife. What bothered me was he could have allowed me know when he wanted to move on we never had an obligation to each other we were just messing around seeing each other. But he didn't he just fussed and it was up to me to read between the lines and with God's help I did. I cried about the lost laying there on the bed I help him get, God spoke to my heart and he said to me you can lay there and cry and except him like this and take this treatment he is not going to leave his wife or you can get up and be strong. You are my Queen and I have better for you, now get up and be strong calmness came over me after this I dried my eyes and got up. There was some anger inside me and I started going through his things, there were a lot of women pictures he was involved with. Also there were pictures of this particular Hispanic woman and a letter he had written telling her how much fun he had making love to her on his bed of rose petals she was there with him a month before I arrived. He had given me a ring when I visited him in Georgia while he was in training for his job. There was a card full of rose petals that she had sent him thanking him for a good time. Also a VCR tape with us having sex and in between the tape space there was his ex wife and him having sex and after that was him and his wife that he is still marry to, having oral sex together, I called my stepfather to pick me up my children were with my mother they had not yet gone to their father.

Before leaving the apartment I trash it with all that was found leaving all on the floor and bed letting him know that all has been revealed now. After this I got myself together yes there was still a little anger but standing strong I returned back to the base and allow myself to feel the pain, and ask the father for help I locked myself up in my barracks room and just prayed. God spoke again reassuring me that I was his Queen and that he has better things for me, he also told me that I am a wife and he does have some one for me but I must wait because in him all things are good and perfect. **James 1:16-17 do not err, my beloved brethren. Every good gift and every perfect gift is from above, and cometh down from the father of lights, with who is no variableness, neither shadow of turning.** While going through this there came along a young man that was stationed with me at Fort Dix in our unit he said he was a minister and he needed me to help him with bible study **Hum!** God has a plan, so we went to bible study every Tuesday night at Charlie Company that's where the entire medical held over lived. We were there to help the sick but God was healing me while attending bible study God 'sword is a healing substance.

Malachi 4:2 But unto you that fear my name shall the Sun of righteousness arise with healing in his wings; and ye shall go forth, and grow up as calves of the stall. God kept speaking to my spirit remember, **Revelation 4:1-4 After this I looked, and behold, a door was opened in heaven: and the first voice which I heard was as it were of a trumpet talking with me; which said, Come up hither, and I will shew thee things which must be hereafter. And immediately I was in the spirit: and, behold, a throne was set in heaven, and one sat on the throne.**

And he that sat was to look upon like a jasper and a sardine stone: and there was a rainbow around about the throne, in sight like unto an emerald. And round about the throne were four an twenty seats: and upon the seats I saw four and twenty elders sitting, clothed in white raiment; and they had on their heads crowns of gold. At that moment I was feeling a lot better and I knew I was healed and once again I was free

CHAPTER ELEVEN

The Evil Plot

While the Minister and I continued bible classes the evil one was plotting he was seeking to destroy the minister's reputation trying to lure him in a lot of things that was ungodly using those that were working with and around us, little did I know he was going through his own heartaches, I allowed myself to be open to the holy spirit of God he has given me the gift of discerning and I could discern those things that were not right and I would warm him, he took heed some time and other times he would fall back. These people would try to work him with promises and gifts sometimes they would work him against me and he would verbally attack me but things turned out alright I never took anything he did or said to heart I would back off, pray and allow God to do his thing. These people would also mark my door with bad words and to make it worse I had to room with one of their friends. While doing a lot of spiritual things this person would say things out of the way around me about me, to those that would listen to her and she would walk around my work table while we were at work. It came to pass the minister and I were both where under attack by this person we had to visit the first Sergeant office, because of allegation s of harassment we were accused of. The First Sergeant knew that this was not true because he himself was a man of God and he knew our reputation concerning our relationship with God, but he had to do the protocol of his job looking into any harassment that came across his desk.

In this meeting was three children of God sitting together in one room along with the evil accuser, it was revealed that she had lied and the enemy was defeated. First Sergeant just threw the case out and there was nothing else said. This person eventually got arrested for prostitution and was sent away God can do all and is in all. **Lamentation 3: 19-26 Remember mine affliction and my misery, the wormwood and the gall. My soul hath them still in remembrance, and is humbled in me. This I recall to my mind, therefore have I hope. It is of the LORD's mercies that we are not**

consumed, because his compassions fail not. They are new every morning great is thy faithfulness. The Lord is my portion, saith my soul; therefore will I hope in him. The Lord is good unto them that wait for him, to the soul that seeketh him. It is good that a man should both hope and quietly wait for the salvation of the Lord. Psalms 37: 1-2 Fret not they self because of evil-doers, neither be thou envious against the workers of iniquity. For they shall soon be cut down like the grass, and wither as the green herb. God showed forth his goodness to us and we saw the salvation of the Lord on our behalf. Coming out of this seven year relationship I made up in my mind to move forward and became sold out for Christ after this decision God placed a special anointing on me to preach and sing his gospel as an Evangelist. For my friend the minister God elevated him to Eldership in the church where he attends, he is still serving in the military and has moved forward with his career; he is now a SGT and is going toward becoming Staff SGT. Me! I'm out of the military and just working for the Lord to the best of my ability knowing that I am just flesh and by the Grace of God I am save and he sustains me with all sustaining power. **Isaiah 27:2-3 in that day sing ye unto her a vineyard of red wine. I the Lord do keep it I will water it every moment lest any hurt it, I will keep it night and day. Psalms 55: 22 Cast thy burden upon the Lord and he shall sustain thee he shall never suffer thy righteous to be move.**

CONCLUSION

It has been my greatest pleasure to allow God to set me aside and to use me, to anoint me, and to inspire me to write this book. This book is written for the unbeliever as well as the believer both can benefit from my testimony. For the unbeliever I pray that the words of each paragraph will touch and be a delivering tool for them and they can step into God's Kingdom and to live free from bondage. For the believer who read s this book I pray they will be heal, and set free from whatever bondage may be keeping them from hearing the voice of the Lord in their lives. Without God we can't do anything but with him we can do all things, in him we live and in him we have our being **Philippians 4:13 I can do all things through Christ who strengths me.** Once again this book is not a novel it is the inspiration of my life that God had mandate for me to share with his people. Thank you for perishing this book I hope you have enjoyed reading how God seen me through. He can do the same for you.

ALL REFERENCE SCRIPTURES WHERE TAKEN FROM THE HOLY BIBLE KING JAMES VERSION:

May God truly bless you and sustain you from all evil.

From the Author

Beverly Ann Swinson

REFERENCE

Revelation 4:1-4
II Corinthians 12:9
Daniel 6: 19 20 21 22
Daniel 3: 22 23 25
Ephesians 6:12
Isaiah 27:2-3
Genesis2:7
James 1:16-17
Malachi 4:2
Matthew 13: 16
Lamentation 3: 19-26
Luke 12:47, 48
Philippians 4:13
Psalm 51: 10-17
Psalms 27: 1
Psalm 121:5
Psalms 55: 22
Psalms 37: 1-2

Psalm27: 5

Proverbs 28:10

Proverbs 28:17

Psalm 46:1 II

Revelation 4:1-4

Romans 8: 28

II Timothy 4:7

I Timothy 6: 12

II Timothy 4:17-18

Printed in the United States
by Baker & Taylor Publisher Services